TRUTH UNTOLD

Truth Untold

MEDITATIONS ON THE GOSPEL

Leslie Houlden

First published in Great Britain 1991
SPCK
Holy Trinity Church
Marylebone Road
London NW1 4DU

The cover shows Giovanni Francesco Guercino's *Christ and the Woman
taken in Adultery*, from the Dulwich Picture Gallery, London. It is the
focus of chapter 8.

Btitish Library Cataloguing in Publication Data

Houlden, J.L. (James Leslie) *1929–*
Truth untold.
1. Jesus Christ – Biographies
I. Title
232.901

ISBN 0-281-04488-0

Phototypeset by David John Services Ltd, Maidenhead, Berks
Printed in Great Britain by
Courier International, Tiptree, Essex

For
Giles and Melanie
Ian and Lesley
Charles and Shirley

Tell all the truth but tell it slant;
Success in circuit lies

EMILY DICKINSON

Contents

Preface

The pieces in this book are mostly sermons preached in various churches and college chapels. They were designed to be heard rather than read, but that makes them easier to read in a meditative way. Sermons are not often published these days, and the preacher would not easily turn into an author if he were not encouraged. Philip Law of SPCK winkled these pieces out of disorderly files and decided which could bear a wider audience. I am very grateful to him for his careful and discriminating help.

It is good for their peace of mind that preachers are not always aware of the extent to which they have only one song to sing. These sermons seem all to be saying: Let's face the Bible with candour and with no forcing or fudging, and then let's see how Christian faith looks to us. There are many fascinating and difficult questions concerning this procedure, and I have tried to write about them elsewhere. But here is a collection of distinct but related attempts at speaking, in the context of prayer, to devout, questioning people who are keen to go further and willing to walk a little way with the preacher.

Leslie Houlden

1

The Place of Scripture

It is, I know, naive of me, but I find it amazing that still after two hundred years and more of the critical study of the Bible and of thought about its role in Christian life in the light of that study, Christians still divide sharply into two camps on the subject. There are those who see it as the authority dispensing the last word on any subject, through and behind any critical tools brought to its interpretation; and there are those for whom it is one factor among others in making Christian judgements, with critical study helping to put the Bible in that subordinate position. Commonly the first group sees the second as faithless, while the second sees the first as benighted, but all the same they often have a bit of a conscience about their own standing with regard to faith. They tend therefore to be less forceful and public in presenting themselves, feeling they are on the right lines but not altogether confident at seeing their way.

I certainly fall into the second camp, though (to be brazen) I do not share the unease about working to hold together faith and enquiry in present-day Christian life, or about using the Bible in that setting. My aim now is to paint, in broad strokes, a particular picture of the role of the Bible in Christian faith. But notice first that the Bible itself, through different writers represented within it, reflects a division or tension not unlike that which I have just described. On the one hand, there is the dynamic principle, of which this passage from Jeremiah 31.31–34 makes a good example: 'Behold, the days are coming, says the Lord, when I will make a new covenant with the house of Israel and the house of Judah, not like the covenant which I made with their fathers … But this is the covenant which I will make with the house of Israel after those days, says the Lord: I will put my law within them, and I will write it upon their hearts.' The message seems to be: in relation to God, don't go for the letter, the outward form; go for the spirit, the witness of God in your inner heart, and be ready to follow where God now leads. New gifts will be available, new levels of fidelity will be demanded. On the other hand, there is the conservative principle: in relation to God, we need to know where we stand and stick to what we have been told. Even innovators can try to enforce that attitude to their own new teaching: 'Blessed is he who reads aloud the words of the prophecy, and blessed are those who hear, and who keep what is written therein' (Rev. 1.3). So wrote a Christian prophet at the end of the first century.

My first point is that to hold to that second principle is likely to involve suffering from a delusion – and the passage from the Revelation of John is a good illustration. In the rest of the passage, and indeed the whole book, the writer proceeds (using Jewish conventions of the time) by taking images and statements from the Old Testament, chiefly Daniel, Ezekiel and Zechariah, and re-minting them in accordance with his Christian belief about Jesus as the climax of God's plan for the world. That is, he failed to stick to his own principle in relation to the old scriptures because he believed that God had given new truth. Despite himself, the writer is moving on to new developments in perception of God and response to him. Unwittingly and unwillingly, he demonstrates, from our detached standpoint, the impossibility of stopping the clock in these as in other matters.

We can proceed to generalize from this: it is in fact inevitable that, in new settings, fresh ways of responding to God arise, and that these should affect traditionally-minded people almost as much as avowed progressives: culture changes; new issues and problems arise which old texts and old solutions never envisaged. You have only to think of modern problems in the realms of peace and war, medical ethics and business ethics to realize how inadequate the Bible is, except perhaps in laying down very general principles, often too general to be helpful.

It does not make things any better when determined Christians try to make the Bible do work for which it is not suited. So an examination candidate was invited to consider an ethical problem. There was a strike at the local works, and in the parish one churchwarden was the managing director and the other was the convenor of shop stewards. What advice should the parish priest give? Simple, said the candidate; Paul taught: 'Slaves, obey your masters'!

That is an absurd example, but you do not have to travel far to find people getting away with examples that are plausible in being only a little less absurd. But they raise a question of method in using the Bible, and people may find it easier to see that the old proof-text approach will not serve, than to see what to put in its place. It is not surprising that there is often a good deal of flitting to and fro between old and new, sometimes (be it admitted) to the convenience of our own prejudices as issues come our way. But in the light of modern understandings of the Bible, chiefly viewing it in its historical settings, Christians need to have a framework in which to think of it. Certainly it is time to move away from the frameworks of the past, whether in traditional Protestantism or old Catholicism. And even if we disagree with the modern approaches, for good reasons or bad, they are nevertheless *there*, on the public agenda. There is no wisdom in continuing as if they did not exist.

In the matter of framework, the fundamental point is not about the Bible itself at all, but about the nature of religious commitment. It is necessary to recognize that faith is faith and not knowledge; that is, it cannot be anchored in unassailable evidence, in documents, popes or any other quarters. Faith is faith, a chosen response of our whole being to God who is both 'other', beyond us, and yet with us and disposed towards us in unrelenting hope.

So though faith has always that character, simply as faith, it is not shapeless or vague; and if it is Christian faith, it gets its shape from Jesus and the long, varied experience that stems from him. Into that experience and life, we enter, drawing upon it, each in our own way, and ourselves enriching it for others. That continuing yet ever changing stream of Christian life in the community of the faithful is the scene of religious reality for Christians, as far as this world is concerned. It is (and has been from the start) the place where human perceptions and words reach up to God and do their best, always fallibly and partially, to say what can be said.

The Bible is not the fount of that life or the determinant of it. God is its fount: the Bible is one important fruit of it, which it took the Church some centuries to achieve. So the gospels, for instance, are not authorities standing over us in some absolute way. They are themselves responses to God as known in Jesus, in principle like our own responses – belonging to their time and place, as we belong to ours; but precious for their pristine quality and their relative immediacy to Jesus himself, as they echo across to us.

So even the Bible, like all other responses Christians have made to God, has a certain reserve attached to it. God, after all, relates to us, as much as to those of old, and we cannot shrug off the hard task of responding now, as the present demands, simply by appealing to decisions of long ago. Anyway, the New Testament itself, in its own great diversity of attitudes to all kinds of questions (like money or marriage or family loyalty), shows that from the start Christians differed in their practical judgements. But all was done in the honest attempt to respond to the vision and call of God illuminated by Jesus – as circumstances demanded.

That is our task too, and it requires all the honesty and hard thought we can bring to it. It requires stimulus from the Bible and elsewhere; but it requires above all quiet fidelity and love for God, who is our sole source and our saving Lord, who trusts us with freedom and seeks our trust in return.

For Girton College, Cambridge, June 1988

2

Word Made Flesh

GENESIS 1.1—2.4
JOHN 1.1–14

—————

If you spend your life lecturing about the New Testament, when you come to preach you have to be careful not to go on lecturing, because the two are not the same. But when you are faced with the prologue of the Gospel of John, there is no harm in letting the two overlap. Any lecture will find it hard not to turn into something of a sermon; and if a sermon is to preach the Gospel writer's mind, it will need to be partly a lecture.

We want to hear what the writer meant us to hear, and the first reading gave us the clue. In what he wrote about Christ, the evangelist wanted us to hear the opening of Genesis. Both start: 'In the beginning'. Both tell of God creating – by means of speech. Like any sovereign, God has only to utter his word and action follows. Both tell of light and life, flowing from him and expressing his mind. Both tell of the emergence of man, God's mind in the form of 'flesh', mere humanity.

And there, of course, the glory and the pathos begin. Adam and Christ both step on to the same path. For both, there is tragedy, disaster; yet the difference is crucial. In the case of Adam, the tragedy brings the loss of glory – that divine splendour which surrounded him, fresh from God's hand. But in the case of Christ, the tragedy (his death) is all glory – it is the climax in the showing of the divine splendour, and it is for us to see: 'We beheld his glory.' That is the chief marvel of this Gospel's way of putting the message; but there are other moves first.

One is that Christ is, through and through, the reflection of God's purposive mind. In Genesis, God creates by way of planting out one item after another, as a gardener gradually fills the bed of empty soil before him. Each item is distinct, and all are distinct from him, even though they express his intention and are touched by his hand. But in the Gospel, all that God does is identified with him, totally expressing him. So: 'the Word was God'; that is, God's mind, whose effects are everywhere, is not something he holds at arm's length from his real nature; nor is it only a partial and perhaps misleading disclosure of his purpose. What he says and means and thinks (the term 'Word' covers all three) is exactly what he is, through and through. God is all of a piece; and if he makes himself known to us, then our knowing is a true knowing. It is limited to our capacity, to space and time, flesh and blood, but we are not deceived. So: 'In him [that is, in the Word] was life and the life was the light of men.' It was God's Word and none other who was 'made flesh'. Christ is the reliable disclosure of the mind of God. When you are involved with God, then it is not less than God you are involved with – not some pale, manageable substitute for him, not a minion who represents some acceptable aspect of his work or character, but God in majesty and fullness of grace and truth. We need, in other words, to be careful before we enter into dealings with him at all. But having decided to do so and found him in Christ, we need not fear being fobbed off with any counterfeit.

Then we should see that the Gospel of John is not much attached to the 'three-act drama' view of the human race's life with God. I mean the view which thinks of creation followed by fall and then redemption. John's adopting of Genesis, putting Christ under the image of God's creative Word, has a striking effect: it makes creation and what we often distinguish as redemption or rescue into a single process or continuous act. It is not that he underplays what we describe as 'fall' – he is well aware of the darkness which menaces the divine light and waits all around. But he holds on to the solid, undeterred continuity of God's purpose. It is not as if God was thwarted or deflected by our race's sin and alienation from him; nor as if only subsequently and as a bright new idea he set about the rescue. No, once more, God is all of a piece, whole and entire, making us what we are to be, from beginning to end.

This goes some way towards removing weaknesses in some of the traditional and mythological pictures by which faith is supposedly illuminated. It focuses our minds on the single fact: the unitary purpose of God. All that we see and experience (we are asked to understand) is set in the single light of his creative love. To look at it in other terms is to risk the fragmenting of life and faith. That is something we often prefer: so that we can take *this* aspect of God, and leave aside *that*. John rules out that device.

Into its reworking of Genesis 1, the Gospel prologue puts, disconcertingly, references to John the Baptist. They seem scarcely relevant and lower the elevated tone of the rest. They strike us as an error of both taste and logic. Why they are there it is hard to say, but there is evidence in the Gospel as a whole that this writer was keen to make plain that John the Baptist was no more than the precursor of 'the real thing'. Perhaps he was beset by fans of the Baptist who made much more of him. But we can permit ourselves to make a little profit from the immediacy-to-life of those references.

We live out our Christian discipleship, not always at the level of high thought or deep prayer, but hemmed in by circumstance, including our limited vision and our blighted prejudice; and the immediate scene is often more vivid to us than heavenly truth and glory. So we can be encouraged by affinity with the Gospel writer, but, having seen in those references most clearly his time-bound, place-bound hand, we must let him show us his real riches: the truth and glory which come from God through the mere humanity of Jesus.

For St Peter's College, Oxford, October 1983

3

The Saving Creator

High up in the arch of the north porch of the cathedral at Chartres, there is a portrayal of God's creation of Adam. The man half squats, half kneels. His head is bowed, his eyes closed as he waits on the threshold of life. Behind him, looking down at him intently, stands the Creator. Acting partly as lover, partly as craftsman, he holds the man's face; moulding it like a worker in clay, waking it like a friend. That is the gist of the carving; but it has two other features.

You can tell it is a portrayal of the creation of Adam because of the sequence in which it is placed. But take it by itself, and you would never guess its true subject at all. You would say it represented Jesus healing a young man or perhaps reviving the son of the widow of Nain. For God the Creator bears all the features of Jesus: strong, young, bearded, robes flowing. And Adam is a youth, not at all the rather mature figure one often seems to see in the stories of Genesis – perhaps in view of the substantial responsibilities with which he is saddled. The other feature is less prominent. But quite clearly behind the Creator stands a cross. It is the background to the whole act which faces us.

We may see this picture as indicating the setting in which to consider the suffering and death of Jesus. The question that arises when you turn to that suffering is: in what context are we to put it? A decision about the context will determine how we react to it.

We can, for example, see it wholly within its immediate setting: a human event in a human story, and so something to be explained by historical investigation, and, at another level, a poignant tragedy, made all the more so by the character of the victim. We shall then be stirred by interest in the causes and the circumstances, so far as we can reconstruct them; and, at the other level, we shall be moved to pity, perhaps to despair at the hopeless incongruity to which the event testifies.

Or else we can shift it to the plane of ideology: it is death for a cause. And we can define the cause in his terms – it is death for the Kingdom of God – or we can translate it into ours, with varying degrees of adequacy and travesty. He dies for human freedom, man's self-realization, or the release of the oppressed. We shall then be moved to reconsider our own loyalties, to measure them against his, and perhaps to identify with his cause.

But the carver of Chartres, making his little masterpiece (and you can easily miss it, as it nestles high up among so many others), caused that suffering to fill the universe. He made Jesus' death the key to the way to see the whole creation. Let us follow him step by step.

First, he challenges what we may call the simple 'three-act drama' view of man's relationship with God: that is, that man was created by God – and that was a good thing; then he fell away from God – certainly a bad thing; then finally he was redeemed through Christ – far the best thing of all. We should of course not take that view in as bald and crude a way as that. No doubt we should say that the three phases are not to be seen as historically successive, but rather as three levels in our relation to the one true God at all times. We stand before him as creatures, as sinners, as restored. With such a perspective we should hope to avoid an obsolete view of the Genesis story, even if it left us a little uncomfortable at having played down the redemptive act of Jesus.

But the artist of Chartres goes further and helps us to transcend ourselves. Creation and redemption are one. The Creator wears the face of Jesus; Adam is the helpless one whom Jesus met in Galilee. It is not the case that creation is passably good, but redemption (a quite separate matter) is much better. Rather, there is one inexpressibly marvellous activity of God, powerful and constant; and Jesus, and all that comes from him, is within that life-giving drive – not improving upon its earlier efforts but working in line with its steadfast purpose and enabling us to interpret it. It is the creative word, says St John, who became flesh – one and the same.

The effect of this first step is quite remarkable. It is to transform the vision we have of the world around us: to break down the barriers between what is to do with God and what rests, flatly, outside his immediate range; to exclude nothing from the scope of our Christian mind; to erase rigid distinctions between the sphere of nature and the sphere of grace. It is not as if God had two grades of love to bestow, two types of purpose to fulfil, like a man who turns his hand to his real interests when his day's work is done.

The second step follows. Both the Creator and Adam are young. Once in a debate on the ordination of women, a speaker announced that he had, from his youth, thought of God as male and aged, and had never seen good reason to alter his opinion. Whatever the usefulness of such a belief in throwing light on the question then under discussion, the carver of Chartres would have agreed on the first count but certainly not on the second. God is to be thought of as young, and so is Adam. God, like man, has much behind him; but he has even more before him. He goes in, not for old, tired ideas and stale policies, but for fresh expressions of his eternal, creative love. We are called to share his preference.

There is a third and final step. The cross stands in the background. It marks not just our redemption, but our very existence as creatures. It signifies not just the cost of our return to God and our adherence to him – but the very condition of human life. What are we to desire? Static happiness, timeless contentment, passionless, uneventful bliss – these are often human aspirations, especially perhaps when we are in a religious frame of mind. But they are not the true shape of God-given reality. That reality is a dynamic process whereby joy is born through pain, love has to be forged through tensions, life springs out of death. The Christian gospel means accepting that as reality, receiving it as a gift not as an imposition to be evaded.

Adam rests asleep, but on the verge of opening his eyes into life. If we can awaken to the truth the carver saw, we too shall be able to receive the life which God bestows upon his creatures.

Formerly published in New Fire *6, 1980*

4

Wilderness Voices

It is sometimes the case with theatrical productions that the whole exercise is designed to set off the talents of one competent performer. When this is the case, it is not always achieved without a certain amount of trouble and tension. Can the principal actor be as good as all that? What is he without the support of the rest? Without them, where is his identity, and, in the light of his presence, where do they stand? Are they merely supporters or do they have an importance of their own?

John the Baptist seems to have functioned in the early Church as a particularly ambiguous member of the supporting cast. If you collect the references to him in the gospels and Acts, you become aware of some embarrassment and uncertainty about what to make of him. Certainly he could not be ignored: clearly there was strong pressure to include him in the Christian story. But it is not easy to see why; for from many angles, he hardly belonged in it at all. He did not survive to be a leader of the Church, and such evidence as there is points to his having given rise to an independent movement, parallel to that stemming from Jesus. His relation to Jesus is presented as indecisive: he is not sure how to understand him, how far to recognize him and support him. Yet, on the positive side, he plays a central part in launching Jesus on the public scene, and his martyrdom foreshadows Jesus' own fate. Thus the gospels present him, no doubt with

14

a mixture of historical accuracy and motives arising from the shifting circumstances of the early Christian communities.

As the gospel tradition develops, he is undoubtedly pressed into a more and more subordinate place. At first, he fulfils the role of a new Elijah, which prophecy associated with the great days when God would show his saving power. But in the last gospel, that of John, he lands up as simply *the voice*, crying in the wilderness. His part is not to 'be' or 'perform' anything very much – simply to speak – to point beyond himself to the central actor. Like the Cheshire cat and its grin, all that is left to him is his voice.

In this portrayal, we see one example of a recurring Christian question: if Jesus is central for our understanding of God and our relationship with him, what about everybody and everything else that plays a part in the matter? How are we to rate their importance? If we rate them highly, will that not detract from the place of Jesus; if lowly, are we not being false to and unappreciative of the plain facts? We shall outline two possible positions and policies, and then point to a third and better way.

First, the plain facts. When we try to weigh up the factors which have produced our faith, we line up a set of John the Baptists – persons, experiences, ideas which have led us to faith and continue to do so. They act as precursors, prompters, preparers of the way. Some of them we are glad to acknowledge and bring into the open. Others are more murky and show us in a less creditable light, or so we feel. We believe not only because we have thought the matter out and decided freely, but also because of elements in our make-up or history which predispose us – friendships precious to us, interests and habits which have come to us, needs we cannot deny.

Without all these supporting actors, where would God be, for us? How should we have known him, how could we believe in him, apart from this escort with which he comes to us – and which colours him for us? So, we may feel, is it really God we know, or some distortion of God, even some travesty? Can we 'grasp' him in some way apart from those factors which press around him? Faith seems so determined and shaped by them all that, bluntly, its self-respect is threatened. It seems inseparable from its cultural and personal packaging.

On the other hand, there is Jesus. There is life viewed and lived with Jesus; and there is life viewed and lived without him. And the two are quite distinct. On the one side, a certain style of living, a certain kind of vision – of God, the world, ourselves – not always easy to define but with identifiable features, clear thrusts and priorities; on the other side, the absence of it all. And this Jesus, we feel, stands in his own right. He is not simply produced by our difficulties or aspirations: rather, he affects and forms them. In terms of the opening analogy, he is, on behalf of God, a one-man company. In this perspective, he needs no John Baptists. If they threaten to impinge upon him, then they are best excluded, or they will spoil clarity and distort the purity of faith.

So how should we see our John Baptists – leave them as wilderness voices or offer them a less bleak and more appreciative role? Certainly we should accept what I call the plain facts – and welcome them. Then we should realize that the policy is not a begrudged necessity – it does not somehow vie with faith, it springs straight out of it. For behind the role of Jesus stands the creative activity of God. 'Who made the eyes but I?' says God to the hesitant soul in George Herbert's poem. The varied means by which we 'see' him, try to 'grasp' him are all his gifts. All are partial, limited, and open to change, by the vary nature of our creaturely relation to him; yet none is valueless if we look to him in the light of his central gift and self-disclosure, in Jesus himself.

We hold to Christian faith, not because we wish to deny the realities of our lives, our histories and personalities, but because we have come to see them in a focus which the figure of Jesus, by all sorts of means, provides. In him and through him, we have found the greatest illumination for our self-understanding. Through him, we have found our way to God. But the varied means by which alone we have done it are also from him, instruments of grace.

There is another good Christian reason why we should resist the conflict and give our John Baptists an accepted place in our estimation. Not only for the sake of God our creator, but also for the sake of the very means of his operation through Jesus. Though Jesus gave to us a life and a death, an offering of himself in teaching and activity, in certain ways he left himself undefined: for instance, he wrote no book saying 'thus and thus must you think', no writing fixed for all time. Rather, it was a case of: 'Here I am, thus I speak: and now, what will you make of it – for *yourself*?' No wonder he taught in parables, content to draw upon his own John Baptists, features of the setting in which he lived, alone making him intelligible.

For *yourself*. Our varied responses have full validity. We welcome every true voice that speaks of him and helps the life-giving play to go on.

Formerly published in New Fire 6, *1981*

5

Truth claims

———

In the background to this sermon, there lies the statement in St John's Gospel, 'I am the way, and the truth, and the life' (14.6); and we focus on the words, 'I am...the truth'. In the Gospel of John 'truth' is a favourite word, insisted on and repeated. So we should begin by asking what the word means *here*. It is, after all, a word used in many senses: a true friend is a faithful friend; a true answer is one that is accurate or correct; a true descendant of someone or a true representative of some cause is one that is valid or genuine for the purpose in hand, just as a true Englishman is one who passes certain tests laid down, perhaps by the Home Office. It is important to know, in a given case, which is in mind. To expect a true friend to be accurate in all his or her speech may be to ask too much; to suppose that a true Englishman will never tell a lie is to court disappointment. To aspire to truth as a laudable ideal does not mean being right all along the way, but rather the opposite, for the ideal takes some reaching.

So what are we to make of the claim that Jesus is 'full of...truth' (John 1.14), or even *is* the truth? The second statement particularly is a strange, unusual thing to say of anybody, and we ought to get it right. To do that is not easy, but I think two things are clear. First, is it not a claim to be knowledgeable and correct about everything, or to be a repository of all knowledge, like some super-winner in a

18

cosmic Master Mind competition. And secondly, it is a claim to be genuine and authentic for the purpose in hand, that is, representing God to us and making available for us a renewed and restored relationship with him. That is what the truth that is identified with Jesus is good for; that is what he gives to us or offers to us. So 'I am the way, and the truth, and the life' may be three forms of more or less the same point: in and through Jesus we are to find access to God, the framework for relating to him and each other, the basics on which we can build all else. He offers, in other words, the status we need in order to be free of the hindrances of fear and hatred and self-concern; a status in which we can proceed to grow and to serve.

That is the good news available for us. But there is a necessary caution to be expressed; for this claim to truth, seen as rubbing off from Jesus to the Church as his agent or to Christian individuals and groups, has all too often been misunderstood. It has been taken to mean precisely what is here excluded: that somehow Christ, and then his followers, are repositories of accuracy and correctness on all kinds of subjects – perhaps matters concerning the natural world (think of Galileo's problems and the furore over Darwin in the last century); perhaps matters of judgement about behaviour or about law; perhaps about the facts involved in religion, concerning the Bible or historical events related to faith. But it is necessary to say that the kind of truth which is identified with Jesus in the Gospel of John does not confer on Christians or on the Church any better information or historical evidence about religion than is accessible to any painstaking enquirer, nor any greater wisdom in making judgements where expertise and attention are required. The Church is given a gospel to proclaim, not a battery of privileged information to communicate. The confusion between these two senses of truth has often done incalculable harm, not least to the cause of the gospel itself. It has led

Christians to resist factual truth or valuable insight, for example about the Bible or Christian history or the life of Jesus, which seems, on good grounds, plain to the enquirer who values integrity.

Indeed, looked at this way, the confusion can easily make religious people and institutions more impervious than others to new factual truth, coming perhaps from secular discoveries, because old, outdated truth seems so bound up with the authenticity of the genuine gospel. We need not worry: the gospel does not profit from that kind of protection. I am not inclined to the dramatic, but I suppose it is true that muddles and failures along these lines have contributed much to the failure of the gospel to commend itself in western society in the present century and before. Christians have often stood on impossible and unnecessary battle-lines in seeking to defend their faith.

Our need then is to be committed to the truth that is Jesus: to the relationship with God which derives from him and to all its benefits; but then to be open to any truth, to as much truth as possible, in every other available way. Open to the 'knowledge' kind of truth about our faith itself, about the Bible and the Christian past; to the 'insight' kind of truth, however it may come to us and from whatever source, when it is a matter of teasing out hard problems of belief or conduct, both private and public – but all in the light of that underlying conviction, that attachment to God and exploration into God which Jesus made available. That is the truth which makes us free, and into which God guides all those who trust in him.

There is one other important factor. God, we believe, is the source of all good, all truth in all my senses; so that having truth as an ideal is one aspect of our quest for God. We do him no honour if we limit his gift to the narrow sphere of our religious tradition: that way we impoverish the tradition itself. It may be that in the modern Church in the West, learning, after centuries of dominance, to make its way in a secular society, the serious division is no longer between Catholic and Protestant: it is between those who see truth from God as present only within the Christian sphere and those who will listen to it and recognize it gladly through whatever hands it is mediated to us, even through God's quite unconscious ambassadors.

For St Barnabas', Dulwich, October 1988

6

Why Not Trust?

JEREMIAH 33.1–4
LUKE 7.36–8.3

All through the history of the Church, Christians have tended to look at the truths of our faith in one of two ways. Some (I suppose the majority) have in practice received them as facts about the universe, to be put alongside other facts: there are the sun and the moon, summer and winter, you and me – *and* God is three in one, there are heaven and hell, and so on. Others – perhaps many in their thoughtful heart of hearts – receive them as invitations into mystery, points at which to focus our gaze, in order to peer and to contemplate, meaning more than they say, 'great and mysterious things which [we] do not understand' (Jer. 33.3 NEB), but by which, so we trust, we may be led through to God.

But this second way often gives rise to a certain unease, even a feeling of guilt. For surely our faith is a revelation and then a proclamation: it is a gift of God and from God to us; and we have a missionary faith – it is a gift to be handed on, a truth to state, to lay down. There is a very great difference between a proclamation (firm and definite) and an invitation into mystery, which easily sounds nebulous and vague. What is more, there is a rich history of people taking the second way to extremes. From the Church's earliest days, there have been Christians who have revelled in a faith of inner, mysterious insights, disclosed only to those (of course always including themselves) with a special gift of perception – able to penetrate the hidden depths. Christian writing is littered with the outpourings of those who feel thus privileged. There is irony in that some of those devoted to a sense of the mysteriousness of God end up claiming to know more facts about him than the rest!

The other way, too, has its dangers, and maybe we are going through a period when the Church is particularly exposed to them. In a prosy age, when words are thought to speak either facts or lies, and to be mistrusted if they do not do either, but point beyond themselves; and in an unbelieving age, when Christians rather tensely feel they must present a definite face to the world; in an age that is both prosy and unbelieving, Christian faith often comes out like a fixed programme of assertions and claims, with sacrosanct ideas and forms of words and policies. No wonder it is so hard to achieve movement and freshness in almost any area of formal Christian statement.

Yet the lack of movement cannot gain its object – which is, presumably, faithfulness and stability; for, willy-nilly, the world (Christians included) moves on, and the old words are no longer digestible, no longer carry the force they once carried, come to mean either nothing very much or else new things; so that change takes place whether one wants it or not.

But, it seems, one must take broadly one of the two ways. Or perhaps one can try a bit of both: perhaps it is a matter of two Christian moods, two aspects of Christian life. There is Christian preaching and witness, and there is also prayer and waiting upon God. There is courage and strength in stating God's word; there is also diffidence before the grace and wonder of God. Two Christian moods, each feeding the other, each playing its part. That is certainly a help; but there is something more fundamental.

We may turn our minds to the gospel story of the woman whose love shows what penitence is and who is met by forgiveness (Luke 7.36–50). The message is clear enough: love and forgiveness, each properly seen, match each other. They belong together, and in our relationship with God neither stands alone. But there is a deeper level in the story. This matching of love and forgiveness is not simply a truth announced, a piece of teaching to put alongside many others. It stems from the very fact that God is as Jesus shows him to be; and that, not just in moral character, but in the very essence of the matter. That is, God is personal, so that he deals with us in terms that are appropriate to the full range of our nature, and not only to certain parts of it (our thinking side, for example, or our formal side, or our religious side – whatever we prefer to present to him). God is personal, and all that he has given us of himself, and so all that we proclaim about him, is under that rubric. Consequences follow.

It is of the very essence of the personal that in relation to others, we never achieve finality or, therefore, total stability. There is always more to find, always new light to be shed; always a new perspective to adopt, always mystery to explore, and always with the attendant risks. But of course, there *is* fixity, there is stability: only, it lies in the sheer fact of the relationship, the gift – God's gift of himself to us. The rest is exploration, movement, freshness, development.

It is a mean view of the Christian faith and life to see it as ideally an assured, unchanging framework, only to be modified with great reluctance and after great heart-searching. Rather, faith is the gift of God's own person as gracious love towards us; and it carries the continual, fresh reception of the gift, for enjoyment and for sharing in a thousand new settings. 'I will tell you great and mysterious things which you do not understand.' That will always be so. But he who tells them is one and the same, dependable and grace-giving. And trusting in him, we can be ready, without fear, for any truth he may give, and even welcome it, the more surprising it turns out to be.

For Westminster Abbey, March 1981

7

The Authority of Jesus

LUKE 20.1–8

My hope is to commend a certain way of apprehending religious truth. It is far from current stridency and it works obliquely. Let us come to it through the story about Jesus' authority. The level of debate between Jesus and the Jewish leaders in the temple is at first sight puerile. They will not say where John the Baptist got his authority; so, all right, Jesus will not say where he gets his. To say the style of discussion is rabbinic helps to explain it for us, but it does not really improve matters. The fact remains that a perfectly proper question, whatever the spirit in which it is asked, receives no answer. Jesus wins on points, but nobody comes away any the wiser and no one appears in a good light. That, I think, is our natural reaction to the story.

Let us try to go further. Perhaps the point is being made that the question was wrong to ask and so futile to answer. They ask: 'By what authority do you do these things?' (Luke 20.2). The question comes in response to Jesus preaching the gospel, it says; that is, it is in reaction to his whole message. In the usage of Luke's Gospel, that refers to the saving truth of forgiveness, joy and freedom, such as Jesus had earlier proclaimed in Nazareth: healing for the broken-hearted, deliverance for captives, liberty for the bruised (Luke 4.16–19). All this total well-being, physical and spiritual, is the substance of Jesus' message. That is salvation – well-being under God and with God.

Now, at this late stage in the story, Jesus preaches his message in the very place above all places dedicated to the cause of salvation. The whole sacrificial routine of the temple, day in, day out, has one single purpose: to perpetuate the saving bond between God and his people and to ensure its consummation in perfect bliss. So it is exactly the place for such a message. But, by the same token, it is exactly the place where the question of his authority to preach the message arises most sharply. Or rather, in this setting, there is an implicit demand that the nature of the question should be decided upon.

In truth, what kind of answer could conceivably be appropriate? In one sense, we, reading Luke, know the answer very well: Jesus' authority is from God – full, high authority that is unassailable. 'Who is it that gave you this authority?' (Luke 20.2) – God himself: 'The Spirit of the Lord is upon me...to preach good news to the poor' (Luke 4.18); so Jesus had started his reading in the synagogue at Nazareth. But that only invites another question: how do you prove that God has given this authority? Then the answer might be: oh well, it can be proved from the old Hebrew Scriptures; or, putting it in later terms, the Church teaches it, or the Pope orders it so, or, often in the history of Europe, the state enforces it. God gave Jesus his authority: that is the answer which you are to accept, because we in turn have authority to speak his truth, or at any rate sheer power to suppress any other answer which has the temerity to be offered.

But the circularity and the nastiness in that unsatisfactory set of reasonings immediately appear. Whatever part they play and have played in backing up religion, these matters do not go to the roots of religious authority. They are carried over from other, secular spheres: from government or the schoolroom or armed forces. And in an age like ours, when authority is widely suspect, it is important for religious faith to know where it stands and does not stand in relation to it. So we return to the propriety of the Jewish leaders' question. Why does Jesus not answer it?

What he does is to puncture their question; to force them away from theory and down to reality – to his message and his person, there, before their eyes; and to John the Baptist, flesh and blood – truth and goodness staring them in the face and overflowing from God's bounty. The fact is that religious truth is self-authenticating – a person 'sees' or does not see. That does not mean that it is foolish, irrational or arbitrary; rather, it is a matter of perception and experience. In story after story in this Gospel of Luke, this is made plain: Zacchaeus the extortionate tax-collector meets Jesus, and from the encounter simply flow both a new vision of things and new action. 'Today', we read, 'salvation has come to this house' (Luke 19.9). Or there is the woman who anoints Jesus' feet in love and penitence, to the scandal of Simon the Pharisee. Healing, salvation result: 'Your sins are forgiven... Your faith has saved you; go in peace' (7.48–50).

What happens in books like this Gospel is not to be left long ago in history or 'over there' inside the covers. It mirrors our lives and then changes them. To read is to involve oneself; that means to risk change. So the Gospel of Luke presents its story of Jesus and invites us to share its perception. It asks whether we (like Zacchaeus and the woman) can see salvation here, find our well-being with God flowing from Jesus, here coming to us in this story. It does its best to create the ethos in which the perception that Jesus is of God will present itself to us. It cannot enforce it or demonstrate it. It can invite it, coax us into it. For those disposed to such a perception, telling by what authority these things are done is irrelevant. If you do not see, telling will do no good; if you do see, telling is superfluous.

Take his story as a whole, and Luke goes a step further: if you do not see, you end up crucifying, obliterating that total good, all that full grace which marked Jesus' every step, every word and deed. So this perception is worth discovering, worth persevering with, lest all that good be wasted.

For Pembroke College, Cambridge, February 1986

8

How many Christs?

In the Dulwich College Picture Gallery, I spent some time with Guercino's *Woman Taken in Adultery*. I found the face of Jesus deeply moving. Young but wholly mature, he searches the accuser's face, daring him to justify himself. He is unyielding in his protection of the woman. Why am I moved? Partly because of the beauty of the composition and of the face; partly because this Jesus chimes in with so many of my deepest attitudes, which, by an indescribably long route, I have learnt from him, but which I am aware of owing to other sources too, elements in my make-up, some of which please me, while others give me unease. He is contemptuous of the accuser's censoriousness and mere moralism; he loathes oppressive cant and unambiguously takes the offender's part. Certainly this is Christ for me: and I'm for him.

But how many quite different Christs does art present to us! Triumphant, gentle, vigorous, ascetic, heroic, weak; Roman, Byzantine, German, white, brown, Semitic, Aryan; you can find them all. Theologians have joined in. We all know that in the nineteenth century they produced lives of Jesus which fashioned him transparently as the embodiment of the age's liberal ideals. Don Cupitt has been telling us that the Christ of the classical orthodox definitions owes much to the imperial ideology of the newly established Constantinian Church, and even if you cannot take that as the whole truth, undeniably he has a point.

And do not the preachers back them up? Christ is not tied, they say, to one culture or time. He is no less Indian than English, no less ancient than modern, one for all seasons. Christ is accessible to *you*, wherever you are. But the preachers had better be careful. Their rhetoric is darkened when we find them so easily endorsing the Nazi Christ, the Christ who blesses English arms, Russian arms, anybody's arms, and when Christ is the standard of the liberation armies, the champion of Marxist freedom fighters, as in other times of anything-but-Marxist kings and fighting popes. For what monstrosities might Christ's name not be invoked now as so often in the past!

What are we to make of this riotously varied gallery? A gallery to which each one of us who follows him could add his little contribution, *his* Christ – or at least his picture of Christ. Is there any way of controlling it all, admitting some but excluding others? And on what basis might it be done, this discriminating between proper and improper claims to Jesus' patronage?

We face the negative side first, then construct the positive. In one sense the whole proliferation is inevitable and unstoppable and it has been going on from the start. When the first disciples of Jesus forsook all and followed him, each found in him something different and saw him in the light of his own personality, background and needs. Each evangelist, we now see clearly, expressed his own view, formed not only by the story he had received but also by his own outlook and the circumstances of his own church. So it has always been: each of us sees his own Jesus, inspired generally by an odd amalgam of those New Testament voices which to begin with were distinct and strong, each singing its song – but by a thousand other influences besides.

In this sense, we cannot claim objectivity for those first witnesses and we cannot think that in certain aspects of the matter they were even attempting it. They had come to faith whereas their contemporaries, also knowing Jesus, had not. And, as I read the evidence (though others read it differently), they were not trying, as we might try, to exclude their own present preoccupations from their way of presenting the story of Jesus. None of this means that their record bore no relation to what Jesus said and did; but it means that they gave what they saw he signified. Nor does it mean that any conceivable book about Jesus would be as much or as little use as, say, the Gospel of Mark. That Mark was not merely setting out to give a full and neutral account but rather a partial and faith-inspired account is not equivalent to saying that his work is pure fiction. It means that the observer cannot help intruding into the picture he forms: it is *his* picture.

On the positive side, I proceed thus. There are, first of all, historical probabilities about Jesus; and as Providence has in these last years put an ever-sharper historical tool into our hands, we ought to use it for all we are worth. So in speaking about Jesus, we can, as Albert Schweitzer showed us at the beginning of this century (in *The Quest of the Historical Jesus*), avoid certain pitfalls – and make certain judgements. We can refrain from affirming that he supported this or that cause because it happens to fire us and has some general backing in some of his sayings. We can, that is, exercise historical imagination with a degree of precision. Moreover, we can outface the style of argument which alleges what he would have stood for if he were speaking among us now: for just as it is nonsensical and unfruitful to ask whether Disraeli, if he were with us now, would or would not support the present Conservative Party, so it is pointless to argue on the basis of what we know of Jesus whether he would or would not have supported the cause of votes for women or Russian dissidents. Everything is so unutterably different. We should concentrate rather, at this point in the discussion, on Jesus as he was on the stage of history, and, as Schweitzer taught, let ourselves be disturbed and moved by him in his own setting, with all its alienness and its power to change our appreciation of our own lives. That itself will inspire us towards certain lines of thought and action and away from others – not by dictating to us but by suggesting to us where to explore. But can we do any better than that and go beyond what history indicates to us? Can we be more confident what policies are of Christ and what are not? Certainly we can; two further paths lie open to us.

First, because it is easy to confuse the Jesus of history with what we assert of Christ now, claiming the former's authority unhistorically for modern action, let us leave the former to be as he was, and for the present turn rather to talk of God. That will clarify our speech about 'the other' aas he impinges upon us now. God expressed himself in Jesus, visibly, once, in specific historical circumstances; his continued and constant expression of himself is in other modes, according to circumstances. Let us then use, for forming our present opinions and policies, the full range of considerations and experiences which open up God for us: that is, in brief, all truth and inspiration that are available to us. Of course we shall look for consistency – God is the God who expressed himself in Jesus – but we shall not make facile transfers and identifications; and we shall acknowledge that, in the matter of perception of the ineffable God, human circumstances, in their constant flux, affect the terms of what may be perceived. We seek then the way of God for now (or, in more technical terms, the leading of the Spirit), not the perpetuation or mere reproduction of, for example, the circumstances of New Testament church life or the judgements of Jesus on issues raised in first–century terms.

Christianity is lived out in a continuing community of faith which is part of the God-given world – and it is opposed to that world only where it neglects or ignores its Creator's existence and love.

Second, we shall then be led to concentrate on certain fundamental thrusts of Christian faith and life – clues for interpreting our experience and so forming our policies: that evil is redeemable, that suffering may be profitable, that love's risks are to be taken, that total generosity is morally absolute, that death is the condition of life – and that life in grace is God's gift to us. None of these provides us with an infallible test whereby we can claim divine support for the ordination of women or the British cause in the Second World War of the abolition of blood sports; but they wholly exclude certain policies which other kinds of Christian interpretation (some kinds of biblicism and some views of church authority for example) have been held to support, and they indicate a certain kind of provisionality about many policies and even good causes; idolatry is to be avoided like the plague. They also leave us work to do – in thinking out how on earth they apply: and so we learn to live by faith.

Formerly published in New Fire 5, 1979

9

The Gift of Faith

MARK 7.24–37; 8.22–26

The reading gave us three stories of healings by Jesus; and I think I should be taken to be evading my duty if I disregarded them. But what am I then expected to say about them? Being not only a preacher but also a child of our time, I know you would suspect another evasion if I did not immediately face the question of their historicity. Certainly, this is about the only question that 'modern man' (including that species as resident in all of us) is interested in. But it is not always good to give people exactly what they ask for, so I shall not evade but deflect that challenge. For after all, it leads to a barren kind of debate: none of us has any privileged access to evidence beyond what is on the page.

So what are the choices? Some of you will believe the stories are straightforwardly true, possibly with a dash of defiance to modernity, because of your prior belief about the nature of Scripture or the person of Jesus. Others will believe, but by way of a little modernizing: they were faith healings, and you had an aunt who was once cured of her arthritis that way. So the stories are, for you, neatly and satisfactorily explained – but at the cost of side-stepping the writer's clearly religious concern. Others will not believe at any price: such things do not occur, the stories are the inventions of the credulous, and the kind of faith they support is unbelievable. Others, finally, will not either believe or stay sceptical, but will take comfort in the words of Mark's Gospel between our second and third stories: that 'no sign shall be given to this generation' (8.12). That is, to think that marvels are a ground for faith is not to begin to understand what it is to know God, trust him and serve him. In other words, events like these, supposing they happen, are religiously neutral or incidental. The heart of the matter lies quite elsewhere. And whatever one believes about historicity, maybe that is the point to settle on, from the point of view of concern with faith, in answer to that modern person inside us who can only think to ask whether they happened or not.

Turn instead to another approach. Turn from what happened (or did not happen) to what is on the page. That at any rate is available to all of us. What we have is stories; stories handed down orally, we presume, for a generation or so, then written down and put in order by the evangelist; and he is the one with whom our contact is immediate. So: can we hear his voice and grasp what he wished to tell us? To achieve that would be a great deal. We must be ready for it to be either what we can easily and gladly hear or what we find hard or uncongenial. He did not, after all, write with us in mind or guarantee to dance to our tune. So what does he say?

The first story, about the gentile woman and her daughter, is undoubtedly the most uncongenial of the three – it is even offensive. However you try and read it as a kind of verbal sparring or game – about the dogs and the crumbs – or turn the dogs into chocolate-box puppies, it is an embarrassing business to us egalitarians and anti-racists. But for the evangelist, no doubt, the story represents a breakthrough – even gentiles can be within the scope of the salvation which Jesus brings, and that is something which could not have been taken in one's stride. The point about pure universality is admirable, but made in a manner firmly of Mark's time and setting, not ours at all (though a persona that understands very well may lurk not far away).

The second story (about the deaf and dumb man) goes better for us, despite the crudity of its healing technique. But the point to fix on needs an ear specially tuned if it is to be heard, an ear as keen as that of the man in the story once he had been cured. Mark uses one word as the clue to the sense of the whole. The word used to describe the man's dumbness, or rather, speech impediment, is rare, and used only once elsewhere in the Bible. It comes in Isaiah (35.6), in a passage where the prophet paints in bright colours the bliss of the coming time when God will set right all ills:

> Then the eyes of the blind shall be opened,
> and the ears of the deaf unstopped;
> then shall the lame man leap like a hart,
> and the tongue of the dumb sing for joy.

This evangelist loves hints of this kind. The word points to the message of the story: Jesus' coming is the time of fulfilment, and this act has meaning beyond itself. God's purposes are being brought to their goal through him – and here in acts such as this healing are the symptoms. So the message is: can you see in Jesus the key to faith, the one through whom to seek God and find him? The story is not, in this writer's mind, about a mere marvel. It is about God, and it makes the religious claim at what is its hardest point – and so also its sharpest point: can you discern God and hold to him in a world which so largely belies him? Is there a new age hovering on the threshold of the world we see – a level of reality below that seen by our normal, clouded vision? And did Jesus truly disclose that level? And was that momentary disclosure really the hint whereby we are to grasp reality – or a heroic, tragic gesture in an alien world?

The third story tells of a blind man who sees, gradually, by stages: as, in the passage that follows, Peter gradually, stumblingly sees the truth about Jesus: 'You are the Messiah', he says, but has to learn reluctantly that this entails death, not simple triumph. So here Mark's story makes its points within his own wider narrative. And again the point is about faith: can you accept God through Jesus on these terms? It is easy for us to underestimate the courage of Mark's insistence here. There were many in the early Church ready to see the resurrection as a victory which effectively obliterated and cancelled out Christ's death. But no, says Mark, Jesus' death is the place to fix your attention. So again, it is the mystery of suffering in the creation of a gracious God; and the word is: face it fully, and you will find within its negative quality the key to positive good.

These stories are all about the true conditions for faith – in one case, the very local conditions of the writer's day; in the other cases, raising issues as live for us as for him. We can be glad of the truthful, brave and undogmatic way in which he raised them by way of story and image. That makes the Gospel of Mark sound like a discussion document. It is not: it is a proclamation of faith, a depiction of a vision of reality. God, it says, is our chief need, and he is hard to discern in a world like ours and in lives such as we have to lead. But he is to be found in Jesus, who gave new life, new vision, new speech, to those willing to relinquish their present hold on things. At great cost, no doubt, we are to see it his way.

For Brasenose College, Oxford, February 1981

10

The Sower

MARK 4.1–20

If I say that I am going to talk about the parable of the sower, you will think that I have set myself a very easy subject and that you are in for a plain discourse. You probably listened to it in a relaxed spirit, for its point seems so clear. Different groups receive the gospel message in their different ways, and, alas, that is to be expected. Nevertheless, the message makes its way – there are those who receive it, and their vitality more than makes up for the others.

But in the middle of that passage, there is one of the most strange and offensive statements in the New Testament. Before I read it, one piece of technical information is in order: 'parable' in English talk usually means a story with an inner, usually religious meaning, and intended to bring out that meaning. In the Bible, it has a wider range, and here, in the Gospel of Mark, its sense is 'riddle', a story or comparison which is mysterious, enigmatic, not clear at first glance. So: 'To you is given the secret of the kingdom of God, but to those outside everything comes in riddles; so that they may look and look, but see nothing; they may hear and hear, but understand nothing; lest they might turn again, and be forgiven' (Mark 4.11–12). It is that 'lest' that causes the trouble. Is Mark seriously saying that the purpose of Jesus' parables is to frustrate the conversion of those who hear them? That God wishes it so? Are parables obscure puzzles of which only the initiates receive the solution, while the rest are meant to remain in the dark – darkness that is black indeed?

Now it is easy to say that the writer puts it in this way because he seeks to explain his experience: that people, many people, were just refusing the precious gospel which was his to convey to them. It is a relief to think, faced with that bitter disappointment, 'Ah, but God meant it so. We have done all we could and should.' But still, the underlying view of religious truth, one not uncommon in Mark's day, is worth pondering: that it is not for mass consumption, not easy of access, a problem to be grappled with, a mystery to be penetrated.

If you turn to the Gospels of Matthew and Luke, working parallel to Mark in this passage, you will find not only that the wording has been altered to ease the offence and the difficulty, but that parables in general have a different character – are more, one might say, what we expect them to be! That is, they are clear and challenging: they hit you between the eyes. There is nothing mysterious about the Good Samaritan story or the Prodigal Son or the Lost Sheep. Hard to act on, perhaps; but not hard to grasp. And their purpose, plainly, is to win those who hear – to give them the chance to turn to God by making the challenge as attractive and clear as could be. So this is another view of religious truth: Here it is, come and get it!

I suppose that Christian faith has continued to present both faces from time to time. On the one side, the straight-forward preaching of the gospel, the evangelistic campaign, the plain course of religious instruction (for baptism, confirmation, or whatever). There it is, the faith laid out; whether they accept it or not, they've heard it, we've given them their chance.

On the other side, a certain reticence, a shying away from giving the impression that Christian faith is easily digested, available in a neat package to be picked up at some meeting or other, or able to be dispensed in a series of instalments like a course in basket-making or tourist's Spanish. It bespeaks a reluctance to take people by storm as if God could be absorbed in a moment. Rather, there is a sense of quiet, gentle attentiveness to God; assimilation of his gift which has, amazingly, come your way; pondering of his truth. And the sad recognition that this path seems not to be straightforwardly possible for all, certainly not in any sense that justifies bludgeoning them with religion or imputing guilt.

Now I suppose temperament is likely to swing us to prefer one of these policies rather than the other, and one may need to exercise self-correction. For there is value in both when you see them as typifying two perspectives on Christian faith and life.

The difficulty of coming to Christian faith is threefold: there is the technical problem of discovering what it is, given the variety and complexity of its forms over so many centuries and in so many present manifestations; the intellectual or personal problem of deciding on its truth; and the moral and spiritual problem of taking it into one's will and one's life. But the threefold difficulty is itself much eased if one grasps the character of the faith involved. Here the two perspectives on religious truth come into view.

First, there is undoubtedly a simplicity at the heart of faith – behind all the complexity of language and concepts, beneath all the twistings of heart and mind. God is my creator and he offers me all good. I have only to stretch out my hand. Christ died for me.

Yet, rightly, I fear some violence to integrity and freedom, some loss of God-given identity. If he truly wills my good, he cannot will my humiliation, if that means the end of my identity. Besides, such violation wins only my superficial loyalty; I cannot, at a moment's notice, summon up the depths of my being, for I hardly know them. His love and truth must seep into me and through me.

So, with the good simplicity, goes the long, hard attentiveness. Only that can do justice to the reality that God *is*. He cannot be grasped in an instant, cannot be *grasped* at all. I see what I am given to see, trust to see more. Recognizing my blindness, I know I must continue in that looking; and with grace given through Jesus as my light, I can gather the direction where more light is to be found. Our seeing is partial, but no less genuine for that: only, it does not do to have too much confidence in our limited vision.

I end, suitably, with a plain parable. Years ago, when I was a college chaplain elsewhere, and the 30th of January fell on a Sunday, the Fellows used to try and tease me into keeping the feast of King Charles. One of them, especially, thought him a martyr for Anglican faith. I thought the monarch rather a disaster. I held out, and kept the fourth Sunday after Epiphany (or whatever it was). But I had not then acquired the insight that came to me, rather negatively, from a Chicago professor: 'I guess', he said, 'that a saint is a figure of the Christian past, whose life has been insufficiently researched.'

All of us have feet of clay, all of us limited vision of God and his truth. It eludes us and is too deep. But not by one whit does that lessen the reality and the need of our love for him and our devotion to his simple and honest service with all our hearts.

For Emmanuel College, Cambridge,
the Feast of King Charles the Martyr, 1983

11

Living with Moral Fragility

ROMANS 7.13–25

I was asked for a title and I said 'Living with Moral Fragility'. Some of you who saw it advertised may (even ought to) have dismissed it as a pussy-footing title: why does he not say sin? What a typical soft-centred liberal ploy! That robust response is attractive: spades should always be called spades, at any rate if they really are spades. But I beg to stick to my proposal, because I want to give an airing to a specific problem, or perhaps a specific way in which the business of being flawed or sinful presents itself. I assume, by the way, that I am speaking to people of high moral aspirations and average success in realizing them; people, therefore, who live with a measure of chronic frustration which you may either take in your stride or find constantly debilitating.

The passage from Romans 7, just read, is of course the classic biblical expression of this predicament. I should say that there are in fact considerable difficulties in interpreting the passage, but I need not show off by going far into them. Briefly, there is a question whether all that moral turmoil refers to Paul's pre-Christian state – in which case it reports a memory but puts him on a different plane from us, for he is not like that any more; or his post-conversion state – in which case one is likely to feel discouraged: if not even Paul could get beyond this muddle of the will, with all his openness to God, what hope is there for us? Or else, perhaps the 'I' of the passage is really 'one', the human animal, in which case it is simply a vivid portrayal of the human condition to which indeed attachment to Christ does offer an intelligible solution, as Paul describes.

I wish to point chiefly to one feature of the passage which will confirm your suspicion of my pussy-footing inclinations, but at any rate gives me Paul as a colleague. As often in his writings, 'sin' figures not as something in us for which we are fairly and squarely responsible, but as something that invades us, that comes at us, and subverts us because we are vulnerable to it, even despite ourselves. Hence my subject: living with moral fragility. Our typical situation is not, as often classically portrayed, that we are deep-set in wickedness, overwhelmed in evil (only in conformity to a theory or in certain moods can we realistically esteem ourselves so); but that we are miserably and depressingly fragile morally, even beyond our identifiable fault, as if somehow got at; constantly failing to round off our good endeavours, to keep precious relationships wholesome, to show love and receive love without messing it up, and failing to think out with any care what our moral priorities should be. Perhaps, above all, these days we are poor at thinking out the interaction between our more personal moral attitudes and those of public and social import. It is amazing how Christians tend to specialize in one side or the other, as if they could reasonably be separated, or perhaps as if no one could be expected to attempt both.

Supposing, however, that we are, according to our lights, morally serious, concerned to be good and for goodness, how are we to view this fragility and live with it? Of course, it is not simply a matter of 'living with it' in the common sense of tolerating it; it is a question of infusing it with vitality, making it creative. I move towards the strong use of 'live' and 'life', as in the Gospel of John. Fragility is ours: it has to become a positive good.

We need to recognize a curious duality in the Christian attitude to sin, at any rate in the case of the averagely sensual human being. It is to hold that sin is on the one hand utterly abominable, serious to the depths, but on the other hand wholly understandable, ultimately even trivial, for God's ready forgiveness awaits us. On the one hand, you might appropriately get into – and stay in – a great state about it; on the other hand, you should scarcely worry about it at all. It is not surprising that, historically, different parts of Christian tradition and different Christian Churches have highlighted one or the other of the two sides which I have so crudely characterized. You can centre all on the dramatic shift, on conversion or adherence to Christ, from darkness to light – leaning partly on one interpretation of our chapter in Romans: then the risk is that you become severely disillusioned and disappointed when the transformation of character proves incomplete. Has God failed one? Has one failed God? (Worse still, you may think that the transformation has gone a great deal further that those around you are able quite to discern!) Or you can centre on a plodding view of Christian life: stumbles occur, nothing much happens, but progress is, we trust, steady if modest, given regular reception of divine forgiveness. There is not much here of the gospel as a blinding light or of anything worth much exultation at all. It is close to being secularity lightly brushed with religion.

It would now be widely admitted that much harm has been done by the dominance in this area of the ethos of the old-fashioned schoolroom and, worse, of the law-court. Paul used it of course, but only to transcend it and show its futility – for God is a judge who acquits the guilty, and whoever heard of such a one? He is, then, a judge only in a very peculiar sense. So much so that we may do better with another language altogether (if we find Paul's irony too strong); with imagery which makes more sense of our fragility, seeing it as a path of life and not of lingering death.

We rest on a base of God's creation of us: we are, in all ultimate senses, his responsibility. Our stumbling and our rising, our growing and our failing to grow are all within that framework. Forgiveness is not, in that case, so much a response we must seek when sin has been done as an essential part of the creative process in which each of us is engaged. It is a term for a perpetual aspect of the vitality and love from God that surround us. Failure is then always deeply serious, deeply sad; but also to be put aside, for hope is unending and God beckons us on. Our fragility is like that of delicate glass: not a sign that we are on the verge of breaking (how negative a view) but a symptom of our beauty as God's creatures, and of the perfection in store.

For Robinson College, Cambridge, October 1988

12

Asking in His Name

JOHN 16.26

I suppose that no prophetic words have ever been more extensively fulfilled than these: 'you will ask in my name' (John 16.26). Whether in the incessant, formal litanies of Eastern Orthodoxy or the terse collects of Western Christianity; whether in the news digests of present-day worship or the urgent supplications of believers and half-believers alike, intercessory prayer has always dominated the Christian scene. In sheer volume, there is more of this kind of prayer than any other, and there always has been; and for many people 'prayer' simply means asking God for this and that, and no other kind of approach to him so much as crosses their minds. And yet, no kind of prayer is more difficult to make sense of, more open to distortion, and more likely to lead to superstitious credulity. It makes a strange picture.

Take it more on the personal level, and you find the same odd combination of features. On the one hand, we may well have grave doubts about the sense in asking God to intervene in specific circumstances in accord with our suggestions: we cannot believe him to operate thus. Grave doubts too about the sense in countless humans battering at God with their petitions, so often trivial, contradictory and partisan. What sort of a system could conceivably correspond to this kind of activity on our part? What sort of a God could it be who would find such clamour worthwhile, and use it, with whatever modification, as the basis of his actions? And how could such a procedure be checked by reasonable people? Once follow that line of thought, and you will soon find yourself wondering whether you can go on making prayers of this kind at all.

Yet, on the other hand, how could our relationship with God suffer the impoverishment of abandoning them? How impossible to exclude from our praying the whole area of our concern and love for other people and their doings, our anguish and hope about the world around us.

So it comes out like this: can we sensibly go on praying? Not sure. Can we stop praying? Certainly not.

Let me suggest certain ways forward. First, praying is deeper than the way we word our prayer. The traditional language of intercession is no doubt based on the picture, appropriate to former times, of our coming to God like servants to a lord, subjects to a king, simple children to a parent. We petition from below, he (according to his discretion) gives from on high. In one way, the simplicity of this picture, so common in the Bible, appeals; it has real religious strength: we are indeed as nothing before God's mysterious majesty, and his ways are beyond us, try as we may to grasp them. But, in another way and by itself, the picture scarcely does full justice to the Christian gospel.

John continues, after the words I quoted at the beginning: 'the Father himself loves you, because you have loved me and have believed that I came from the Father' (John 16.27). And the sense of the whole passage is that God raises us to a position of intimacy such as Jesus has – not servants but friends. Interceding, petitioning (from very much below to very much above) may not be the best style, the best wording, for bringing our love and concern for others into our speech with God. We may do better to see ourselves as claiming a higher place in working for God's cause, striving to form and carry out his purposes. We are his people, engaged in his work and, however we put it into words, what we seek is not his extraordinary and partisan interventions, but rather his steadying and empowering presence, in order that love may win its way. Even if improving the words, especially in public worship, is like moving mountains, at least we can improve the picture with which we go about our praying.

Secondly, therefore, it is a distortion when intercessory prayer gets isolated from other ways of expressing our relationship with God. Engage in that kind of praying alone, and you can scarcely avoid falling into either disillusion or superstition. We come to God with a wider trust, a more general adherence. We do not just seek his gifts, much less his favours; we give ourselves to him simply because he is our God: 'for his own sake alone' is the key to our attachment to him. That is why, when we are engaged in the liturgy of the Eucharist, the problematic side of asking God does not really strike us: the context, rich in variety, widens the whole matter. In that context, we express the total range of our life in relation to God as we know him through Jesus. Intercession can bear a place within it, but it does not dominate.

So, finally, asking, says the text, is to be 'in my name'. Christian prayer is not a simple, unreflective human asking – voicing whatever comes into one's limited, selfish head. It bears the marks of Jesus. It is filtered through what Jesus stands for. That link with him, with the Jesus of the cross, who gave himself, shouts out against any kind of crude prayer, which seeks simply to remove the troublesome areas of our own or others' lives. 'In my name' means a readiness to work through the realities of the given world, a willingness to shoulder the burden of God's cause, cross and all. 'In my name' speaks of a kind of gladness at living with the world, but because of him finding it transformed to our sight: no magic erasing of disabilities, no special escapes from reality for any favoured ones; but a new joy and strength in facing everything with his generous love and so finding it made quite different. 'In the world you have tribulation; but be of good cheer, I have overcome the world' (John 16.33).

For the University Church of St Mary the Virgin, Oxford,
May 1981

13

Happiness and Blessing

MATTHEW 5.3–12

When the translators of the Jerusalem Bible chose to start
the Beatitudes in the Gospel with 'happy' instead of
'blessed', I hope they had sweated blood over the question.
I do not know what decided them, but I imagine they felt
that 'blessed' was too archaic and fossilized in religious talk.
But their hope for modern accessibility was misplaced. If
religious terms have become meaningless, the culture being
so secular, then you have to stop translating the Bible
altogether – not much good tinkering – and perhaps you
should just recite it, in deep cultic mysteriousness, in Hebrew, Greek or perhaps Latin, whichever is understood least.
But if shreds of religious and Christian awareness persist,
you can afford to strengthen them by keeping their language
going: up with 'blessed', down with 'happy'. Use the right
word and you may come to feel the flavour of it.

I say 'blessed' is the right word, accessible or not. *Maka-
rios* is the Greek, and it *can* mean 'happy' or 'fortunate'.
Occasionally it does in the New Testament, as when Paul
gloomily judges that a woman who has lost her husband
will be 'happier' if she stays a widow and does not remarry.
But wherever religion or God is anywhere around in the
context, then it's 'blessed'.

'Happy' is the wrong word in the Beatitudes because it
sends you scuttling into the wrong paradox. Happiness is
inescapably close to contentment or cheerfulness: and

51

'Happy are those who mourn, for they shall be comforted' (Matt. 5.4), becomes impossibly puzzling or downright misleading. 'Happiness' can come at you from any quarter, often surprisingly, but it is a human gift. God may be its ultimate source, and if you are a believer you thank him for it; just as you say grace at meals. But it does not immediately set you in a rich context of religious reflection; and you can share it readily with unbelievers, even in marriage and close friendship – just as you can eat with people who dive straight in like the cat.

But the Beatitudes are all paradox; only it is paradox of a kind that makes both the happy and the unhappy sit up. 'Blessings' are God's business and come only from him. Even when an atheist says 'Bless you' as you sneeze, we must take him to be lapsing momentarily and inadvertently into theism. And when a priest is said to bless people, he should recall that he does not really act in his own persona, but backed by Another.

So what sort of surprise is it that the Beatitudes put before us? It seems all right to say that it is the pure in heart who will see God, but the rest fly in the face of experience. Whenever will the meek inherit the earth, whatever that might mean? It is only the pushy who seem to get on the track of it.

At this point, New Testament scholars come in unhelpfully and say that the Beatitudes are eschatological in their reference. They speak of a great new order which first-century Jews, then Christians, believed God would bring about. In it, earthly values would be reversed; and no doubt the aspirations of the have-nots went into these statements. Jesus and his followers were full of this outlook: it was the very stuff of their message. But that is no good to comfortable us, though it still gives liberation theologians and their oppressed friends hope – hope against hope, we might say. In any literal sense, the expectation in the Beatitudes was disappointed, and people spiritualized them for comfort and for intelligibility. Even the Gospel of Matthew did it already, while Luke's parallel resisted it: 'Blessed are the poor *in spirit*', put Matthew (5.3); 'Blessed are you poor', said Luke (6.20). 'Blessed are those who hunger and thirst *for righteousness*' (5.6), wrote Matthew; 'Blessed are those who hunger' (6.21), said Luke, with his feet on God's good ground.

So what can be done with the Beatitudes? The choice is ours: we can at least gaze at them as from afar, with nostalgia for what never was, but might have been. That might, at any rate, shame or inspire us to have a preference for and to work for a society where the poor and the hungry and homeless get a sniff of needs met – and it might enable us to see that work in terms of a God-purposed world, for 'blessing' implies a context centred on him. That restraining of our instinct to be and to stay wealthy possessors means, admittedly, attending to Luke's socially troublesome Beatitudes rather than Matthew's more religious ones.

But Matthew's Beatitudes too are revolutionary. Only, they will urge us to a total revision of the values and perceptions by which we all get on along the world's accepted paths of achievement. And even if you cannot manage that total reversal, at least you can know its demand and throw yourself on a loving God in discontent and penitence. Then there would be real learning about the life of faith in which we are saved by the skin of our teeth.

Reading the gospels is not like reading a handbook for life. It is exposing yourself to such an alien picture of things, where poverty is preferable to wealth, death the only gateway to life, and suffering somehow the key to getting things right – such an alien picture that we may be shocked, again and again, into the world of God's strangeness, and thereby be filled with blessedness.

For Magdalene College, Cambridge, February 1990

14

The Snares of Wealth

MARK 10.17–30

———

Some years ago, taking on an unfamiliar role, I was sent to review Alec McCowen's recitation of St Mark's Gospel at the Mermaid Theatre. I remember three things about the performance. First, of course, that it was an amazing feat of memory. Second, how bizarre it felt to have to break off for ice-cream after the story of the transfiguration. And third, the response of the rather comfortable middle-class audience of which I was a member. Only once was there evidence of our being stirred to the heart. I noticed no sign of tears or sighs at the story of Jesus' death, no horror at his betrayal, no astonishment at his great deeds. All these things we knew well and (alas) took in our stride. But at 'How hard it will be for those who have riches to enter the kingdom of God' (Mark 10.23), a ripple went through the whole audience. That got us on the raw and we shifted uneasily in our seats.

Here, going with the story of the rich man's encounter with Jesus, is a statement which is universally menacing, infuriating and haunting. Menacing because it subverts the hopes if not the present state of practically all of us; infuriating because its demands seem quite beyond us; haunting because we cannot on that account just carry on as if we had not heard it.

First, then, it is universally menacing. As we read, many may feel exempt, whether for good reason, as it seems, or out of that general human conviction that the rich are other people. But the story has every one of us in its sights, for it is really about renunciation, readiness to enter a crisis of abandonment. 'Great possessions' by some standards we may not have, but we have our own adequate nest; or we have the prospect of it within a measurable time; or we have the hope and the lust for it, with its security and assurance. Spiritually, in the heart, all three are much the same; and they are poles apart from the spirit of the story. The story threatens us all.

But also, secondly, it is infuriating, because its demands are beyond us. It is maddening to be made to feel guilty and yet have no way of discharging that guilt. For what, supposing we have the best will in the world, can we realistically do in response to the threat of that story? If it embodies what 'following Jesus' involves, had we not better give up the pretence? We cannot reasonably put ourselves and our families on the streets, and even now, with all its lamentable gaps, the welfare state would in many cases pick us up sufficiently to bring the story's challenge into play once more. Unless we are very determined, or very ingenious, or (much more commonly) unfortunate, it is not easy for us to meet the challenge at all adequately.

Nevertheless, it remains haunting. For we are bound to feel that it is very close to the heart of what Christian commitment involves. We cannot cheerfully relegate it to the scrap-heap of outmoded imperatives. It is one thing to laugh at St Paul for apparently insisting that women wear veils in church. Many of us may indeed have our list of traditional Christian rules which we regard as no longer compelling or convincing. And in general terms, a faith, whatever its claims to continuity, adapts to new situations. But it would be a strange Christian (though they exist) who said straight out that the story of Jesus and the rich man had now no force at all. Such a one would seem to have given up the whole moral identity of the gospel. The story haunts us. Yet, from top to bottom, this imperative which we dare not discard is in effect ignored by Christian people with a recklessness and a universality that are surely unrivalled – except in the case of the comparable injunction to renounce family ties. Churches hot in pursuit when it comes to Jesus' teaching on divorce, and zealous in endorsing love of neighbour and the duty to be merciful and humble, accumulate wealth by the million and enlist the support of the rich at every opportunity. These things they do (and we all in our measure do) virtually without turning a hair – and what's more, we always have.

For the attempt to massage the story of the meeting of Jesus with the rich man into a prettier shape goes back almost to the start. At the end of the second century, it was already read as hyperbole: what it really meant was, give alms generously and be detached from your possessions. You may feel this is a cheat. It is after all less painful to give away 10 per cent of one's income that to ditch the lot; easier to meditate on God coasting along in one's Porsche than to give the thing up out of commitment to him. Many of us who shrink from the one might have a shot at the other.

It is, moreover, clear that even before that story was first written down in the Gospel of Mark, Christian congregations in Greek cities were compelled by circumstance to rely on the generosity of their richer members. Within a stone's throw of time after Jesus' life, practical living had already created conditions in which every element that I have pointed to in relation to this story was already in place – in effect, its impossible idealism. Our predicament is not new.

So, looking back, we try to put it where it belongs – in the short-lived context of Jesus' ministry, or else that of his first followers, perhaps living in villages in Galilee where possessions were more dispensable that in the city. They awaited eagerly the gift of God's Kingdom when riches would anyway be irrelevant; and gladly they wagered on its coming by giving up all, loosing all ties with possessions and family, everything that could hold them back and blur their vision. Of course, not all was abandonment and loss: as Mark indicates, the Christian group was one's new family, the household of God. Its no doubt modest resources sufficed to sustain life in the brief meantime. The costly gesture of abandonment once made, there was indeed a new security.

The hope for the Kingdom of that first Christian springtime was of course not realized, and perforce harsh reality compelled a softening of practice: the rich came in as benefactors; Christians helped one another to live on a modest competence; and they became devoted to the virtues of family life. (Whatever the history books say, the Mothers Union and the League of Mary were effectively founded not in the nineteenth century, but in the latter part of the first!) But the story remained: no longer 'real', but to threaten, infuriate and haunt.

Is that then all there is to say? To put the story in context is to neutralize and decontaminate it. As I defused the bomb, you may have felt relieved: relieved of even having to find the story haunting, let alone threatening and infuriating. But I hope you felt instead that you did not want me to get away with it. For, putting it bluntly, even when they cannot for the life of them see how they are to follow him, Christians cannot be content to lock Jesus away in his first-century glass case, there for us to examine, but unable to reach out and touch us.

The difficulty is, I think, extreme; but we may take up these reflections: first, the story is about self-abandonment. It makes the same point as sayings in the gospels about the need to give up life if you would save it and die if you would live. Those statements are all at the heart of what the Christian religion, in the end perhaps all religion, is about.

The life of faith is a never-ending quest for the realization of that abandonment. It is an endless giving of the self to God, in comparison with whom all else is but dross.

Secondly, the story is also about possessions – about money and about things. It is therefore the antidote to religious delusion. Religious people deceive themselves a great deal by their delight in piety and their sense of being on the right track; and on no subject do we wear more layers of hypocrisy than on this. The story of the man who would not give up his possessions brings us up short and then makes us act, in whatever degree or sphere is open to us.

Thirdly, the story faces us with the impossible, but it need not on that account infuriate us; nor need it merely – and ineffectually – haunt us. Certainly it can take us well beyond the question it raises about a Christian's attitude to wealth. It may teach us that we cannot make headway with God on the basis of our achievements. A discharged conscience is a delicate luxury which, in this as in other matters, we cannot even hope for. The command to sell all and give to the poor was never a compassable command designed to rearrange the economy, even though on many grounds the economy may desperately need rearranging; just as the blessing of Jesus on the poor does not consist in their becoming rich but in their receiving the Kingdom of God. What is at stake is recognition of the impossibility in any circumstances of our being anything but 'poor' before God: poor – but therefore empty and ready to be filled with his love and strength. Poor, and therefore free, to be as clear-sighted and as generous as, by his grace, we have it in us to be. 'How hard it will be for those who have riches to enter the kingdom of God.' But, the passage goes on, 'all things are possible with God' (Mark 10.27). There is a necessary simplicity at all levels in our relation to God, a 'poverty' whose practical integrity each of us must learn.

Truth Untold

The Gospel of Mark says of the man who went away, for he had great possessions, that Jesus, looking on him, loved him. The bearing of those words is typically enigmatic; but they may give us comfort on many a dark and puzzling day.

For King's College, London, January 1987

15

The Community of Christians

I CORINTHIANS 1.18–25

My church day has been one of contrasts. This morning I celebrated the Eucharist in a church in South London where everything was about as run-down and simple and difficult as you could imagine. Everything uncertain and unstable: a small, almost leaderless congregation, struggling to survive, amid divisions and weakness; yet also a Christian presence in a problem-ridden environment, as deprived and grisly an estate as any in the land. Tonight I am in Cambridge, accepting your invitation to preach. I shall not attempt to list your characteristics. You can rehearse them for yourselves and feel the difference.

The lesson gave us Paul's view of that earliest Christian congregation visible to us with any degree of clarity, the congregation in Corinth in the fifties of the first century. It is a view which always causes a certain embarrassment when put before an academic audience. For is Paul not saying that brains and high culture are an obstacle to Christian faith, and that in truth Peckham rather than Cambridge is the place to see the meaning of Christ?

I am not being evasive or polite if I say, no, not, I think, quite that. The congregation at Corinth was not as monochrome as appears at first glance: not *many* wise or well-known had been called to faith, but *some*, it seems, had. They were a mixture – Peckham, Cambridge, if not a dash of Belgravia too. And Paul himself displays too much rhetorical talent as he does his depreciating turn to be entitled to condemn intellect pure and simple. No, what he condemns is not brains but wisdom: that is, in his terms, a kind of spiritual insight, proudly held, pursued for its own sake; one which found unedifying and so by-passed that central disturbing fact of Paul's gospel – the death of Jesus.

With all his paradox, weaving in and out, that is the subject and point of Paul's message. The death of Jesus by crucifixion is the expression and sign of God's power and wisdom. It is the signal for a whole reversal of values, religious values included. More than that, it is also comprehensive, it is all that Paul preached. He 'decided to know nothing [else] among [them]' (I Cor.2.2). Further, this message can unite rich and poor, clever and simple. It levels and unites, for everybody is challenged, in their sheer humanity, by such a manifestation of God's power. Not moved to pity, so much as disturbed in their assumptions in stable existence, both social and personal: for what kind of a world is it, when value is attached to an event like this, a paltry criminal's death?

That is Paul's point as he addresses the rather heady and otherworldly religiosity of the Corinthians. He aims to bring them down to earth, to make them face realities. But in what terms can his words still impress? Impressive rhetoric, certainly; but is the sheer rhetoric too strong? Has it carried Paul away, made him overstate and unbalance things? Or else, is he addressing a situation of purely local interest, treating an illness from which we do not suffer?

In one way of course he is. Proud and speculative religion has its examples among us, but it is not, surely, the most serious threat to most Christian lives. But diversions from the central message, the God-given proportions of our faith, are legion. It would be tedious to specify at length, and the diversions are different for each of us. But when I survey the topics which most agitate the Church at large, I find it hard not to see many of them as just that: corporate diversion from the central message as Paul defined it.

So let us share Paul's great virtue, which at this point is sheer clarity of spiritual vision. 'I decided to know nothing among you except Jesus Christ and him crucified.' And what is the backing for that? That he is 'the power...and the wisdom of God' (I Cor. 1.24). This strange, unlikely act is God's way of achieving change and fostering understanding among us. It does it not so much by making a case as by causing a shock. Let us consider three (among many) aspects of that shock.

First, it bears on our understanding of power. If, as Paul says, the death of Jesus is the symbol and expression of God's power, what does that tell us about our estimates of human power, and in what directions does it urge us to expend our energies? How does it amend our sense of what is worth working for?

Secondly, it bears on our understanding of love. If God's concern for us is exemplified in this extraordinary, perplexing and shocking way, what are we to make of our attempts at loving and redemptive acts? What styles and degrees of generosity may not be required of us? If true moral wisdom lies along this path, can we find the will to follow it?

Thirdly, it bears on our understanding of suffering. For if God is intent to make much good of the suffering of Jesus, and if Paul as the apostle of Jesus sees his own vocation as expressed in weakness, in fear and in trembling, then must not we pursue relentlessly the creative value of ills that afflict us? In all these ways, my Peckham Eucharist and Cambridge Evensong converge to a unity of obedience to the call.

For Queens' College, Cambridge, February 1981

16

Maximizing the Talents

MATTHEW 25.14–30

It is today what Anglicans, at least, know as Bible Sunday. Present attitudes to the Bible are often strange and contradictory. People can combine great respect for it in theory with great practical neglect of it – and wariness in getting too close to it and finding out too much about it.

If, like me, your job is to study and to teach the New Testament, you sometimes find yourself treated like a terrorist device: if allowed to do your stuff, you might go off and cause damage to faith and to cherished opinions. And sometimes there is a kind of conspiracy. One evening I was giving a talk to a parish group, and we were standing round before the meeting began. The Vicar came up to me and said, 'Do be careful what you say. I like the kind of thing you say, but my people are easily upset by new ideas about the Bible and their faith.' A minute later, a member of the group came up and said, 'Do be careful what you say. We like the things you stand for, but the Vicar easily gets upset by new ideas.'

My general aim, then, is to push that fear away by saying what modern Bible study sets out to do. It is neither more nor less than to let the various writers represented in the Bible speak for themselves: to hear what they really had to say rather than what we would like them to have said or what immediately strikes a chord with us. That sounds a modest enough objective. In fact it is a task of considerable difficulty and delicacy – in two different ways.

There is, first, the sheer technical task of trying to *place* a particular bit of the Bible (this book, psalm, story or letter) in its original setting: to see as vividly as possible what, in that far-off time, its author would have meant by these words, this way of putting his ideas and his message. It involves a kind of journey in imagination from our own day and our own society with its assumptions and problems to that of another time and place – in which Jesus lived; or Paul wrote to Christians in Corinth; or Mark first took up the pen to write the story of Jesus as God's chosen agent for our salvation. To make that journey with some success is, surely, the great achievement of modern Bible scholarship.

But there is not merely a technical task. There is also a question of our humility and adaptability. If we want to listen to the biblical writers on their own terms, then we must reckon that there is quite a chance that their words will not speak directly to us or chime in with our views and beliefs. There is a long history of Christians making the Bible, this part of it or that, mean what they have wanted it to mean – reading it through spectacles of their own making. Hearing it on its own terms can often be a shock and a challenge to cherished beliefs. It can also be, initially, a puzzle: how can I, if at all, learn from this statement, this story, which seems to belong to such an alien world? The learning may well be hard and indirect: our heart or will prompted to move in directions we should not have thought of, compelled to think new thoughts about God and about serving him; forced to see Jesus in a new and perhaps disturbing light. For he, above all, very easily gets shaped in our minds into a congenial and helpful image which may neglect most of what he stood for. Churches and individuals have a great need to hear the authentic voice, so far as it is available; and the candid return to our roots, especially in the witness of the earliest Christian writers in the New Testament, will press us into more adequate directions of thought and action, by at least disabusing us of the old interpretative myths. Our forefathers, lacking modern historical skills and historical sensitivity, had every reason to reach understandings of Scripture congenial to them. Historical awareness makes that excuse unavailable to us.

Let us, by way of example, try to hear what the writer of the Parable of the Talents, read in the lesson, wanted us to hear. Think: on a particular day, some time in the late first century AD, the writer of the Gospel made the deliberate decision to set that story down. That means that it must have been important enough to him to contribute to his picture of Christian understanding and life. What then did he want his readers to see and hear?

The outline of the story is clear enough; and it is at first sight discomforting and threatening. The man hands out his property to servants and goes away. They use the gifts received in contrasting ways: some use them productively and profitably; another, acting it seems both foolishly and perversely, does nothing with his gift at all. Then comes the reckoning, and rewards and punishments are dispensed.

The meaning has always seemed clear, so much so that its interpretation has even contributed a word to our language. A talent in the story was a unit of money in the time of Jesus; by way of this story, the word has come to mean a skill or accomplishment which is just 'there' in our make-up – an unsolicited gift in our personality. So the story seems to say: make sure to use the skills you have been given – and you will be judged accordingly. If you can sing, sing away furiously and God will be pleased with you. Stay tuneless, and your fate will be unimaginably terrible. It seems to be a story that is not very profoundly religious at all, just rough-hewn moral wisdom; and it sounds excessively frightening in its rigour. Can it really be, can anyone have thought, that if you are good at tinkering with cars and fail to do it, you will be excluded from heaven for ever?

So then, let us attend to the story afresh and see what it has to say. Why did the evangelist put it into his book?

We know that at the time he wrote many Christians were acutely aware of living in a strange, ambiguous time – suspended between the lifetime of Jesus, whose whole career had changed everything for them, and the full revealing of God's purposes when what Jesus stood for would come right out into the open. It was a situation fraught with difficulties and temptations for Christians. How should you react in your waiting? Should you just hold on, passively, awaiting God's good time? Should you just sit, confidently, in your Christian enclave, basking in the light shed by Jesus' teaching, and his death and resurrection? Or should you get out and do something? But if so, what exactly should you do? What was worth embarking on? How should you see your task in life?

The story is both decisive and practical. It is vital, it says, to see that there is productive work to do. And to do what is to be done, the Master's gifts are to be used. The master in the story is of course a thin disguise for Jesus. So the Christian's raw material is what Jesus has left behind – his teaching, his 'image', the marvellous story of his life, death and triumph. That is the legacy for his followers to keep, and not, I think, a propensity for singing or car-tinkering. It is a legacy not for mere keeping or being grateful for, but for using, for making something of, for working out and spreading around, for applying in real life, however it comes to you. In other words, the message is about making sure that everything that is yours from Jesus really penetrates your world and colours it from end to end. Then, of course, your reward follows; not crudely, as a bonus for good conduct, but naturally, as the outcome of the situation that has come about, including the style of people you have come to be. For what could be more decisive for our relationship with God than the way we have set out to live in the light of all that Jesus has made available?

We live, as the story's first readers lived, in a strange, in-between time. We are suspended, as Christians, between our knowledge of God through Jesus, which stands somehow behind or above us, and a plain and full perception of God's purposes. God is, in that way, both clear to us and yet obscure. He gives his gift, yet remains withdrawn. In the space between, we have responsibility – and that is fearsome; but we also have freedom and opportunity – and that makes the heart dance.

For Westminster Abbey, December 1985

17

A Kingdom not of this World?

JOHN 18.36

For preaching this sermon, I received two pieces of advice. I should be somewhat provocative; and I should speak on spirituality today. Many people would think the two pieces of advice incompatible, for what subject could be less provocative than spirituality? If you go to hear someone speak on 'Christianity and Politics' or 'the Theologian and the Pew', you have only yourself to blame if you are provoked. But 'Spirituality Today' arouses different hopes: of encouragement, perhaps, of something benign, even sedating.

However, my text has served for dynamite in its time, and anyone with a historical memory would hesitate to use it, for example, in preaching before the General Synod. A sermon on 'My Kingdom is not of this World' was preached by Bishop Hoadley of Bangor in 1717, and aroused such fierce reaction in Convocation that the King dismissed it, and it never did business again until 1852. No words of mine are likely to be so long-term in their effects.

Spirituality, as a subject on its own, is a curiously modern interest. I note that the sense in which Christian people now use the term – to refer to the quest for God in prayer, the devout life – has not yet got into the dictionaries. There are signs that we have become more self-conscious about it, perhaps clutching after it because we find it elusive and difficult, though deeply attractive. We know there is something vital there, but it is not easy to grasp it or to feel one is satisfactorily getting on with it. So we itch for it, go after it – lest we should lose the skill of it for ever; or because it seems to offer a last hope in a hard world.

It helps if we put the matter into context. To go back to the beginnings of our faith witnessed to in the New Testament: it would be absurd and artificial to try to isolate the spirituality of the first Christians from other matters, such as beliefs and ethics. There is, at that stage, a single, all-embracing commitment which affects everything: how you think, how you behave, how you pray. It was all of a piece. So it was for many centuries: there was the single, all-embracing response to God, coming out in belief and prayer and conduct, each nourished by and intertwining with the others. It was long centuries before people wrote much about techniques, or prayer as a subject in itself.

Then, just over two centuries ago, comes the gradual capture of theology and ethics by secular thought. Theology, as a study, has become less and less the personal quest for God, and more and more the detached study of ideas about God – their history and their validity. What with that, and the increasingly secular world in which Christian life is set, it is no wonder that Christian people feel somehow cheated, and protest: whatever being a Christian is about, it cannot be exhausted by the worldly aspects of the Church's life or by the study of thought about God or the Bible. There must be an inner spring of desire for God; and we simply must discover the place of that spring within ourselves and let it irrigate our lives. So we attend to 'spirituality'. We read books to help us to pray (not to think or to act as Christians, but specifically to pray). We go to gurus, for advice about our souls; we go on retreats, where prayer is, again, often separate from thought, study and action. We cultivate ourselves as praying persons – for understandable reasons and with admirable intentions. We want to nourish something inside ourselves which seems starved, and which our instincts tell us is the key to our integrity as Christian people, perhaps because other possibilities have failed us. Behind doubts and difficulties and in the midst of a distracted and worldly existence which presses upon us, this, we feel, must be safeguarded at all costs. And if there is a charge of escapism over our heads, well, so much the worse: there is much to be escaped from.

Yet there is something phoney about this isolating of spirituality. The precious seedling is easily treated as a hot-house plant. Our 'spiritual life', as we call it, does not then mesh with the rest of life. Prayer comes to march uneasily with the understanding of our faith, or with the conduct of our lives and the arranging of our relationships. We are, many of us, pressed into being divided people: Christian in basic allegiance and in hope and aspiration; very like our unbelieving neighbours in many of our assumptions and ideas and priorities, despite all our praying. Partly it is not our fault: we are victims of the process I have described. But the question then is: can we do better?

The statement in the Gospel of John, 'My kingdom is not of this world' (18.36), is often misunderstood. Bishop Hoadley took it to mean that the Church should forswear all visible, earthly power and authority; and the English clergy did not like it when they thought what it would mean for an established Church in Hanoverian England. In our own day, politicians quote it, as a knock-down text, when they want to deter the Church, or rather clergymen, from making utterances on social and political subjects. Real life, including politics, is one thing, they say in effect; religion, spirituality, is another – and their sphere is the inner self and the other world. But the gospel statement means no such thing. 'My kingdom', Jesus says, 'is not of this world'; not in the sense that it has nothing to do with this world, but that it is not grounded in or confined to this world. Its power-base, its impulse and source, are elsewhere – in God himself. But, coming from him, that rule of God spreads everywhere, colours everything. There is no inner realm (in the Church, or in our souls) where God's writ specially runs. There is only the world of God's creation, in every corner and aspect of which we must learn to know and serve him.

Sermons should have a message, and it is time to state today's message plainly. First, there is much inside us and much in our society which presses us to cultivate our spiritual life (as we call it) as a thing apart. We may be encouraged in that direction by escapist tendencies or by the difficulties in leading more integrated lives as Christians – perhaps by what seem like insuperable problems in belief or behaviour: in the interior self, can we but nurture it, we can be fenced off from such matters. Nevertheless, we find it unsatisfactory, for the excellent reason that to isolate the spiritual quest in this way is artificial. Instead, whatever the hardness of it, we need to seek God in all parts of our experience and all areas of our possible obedience – in the honest understanding of Christian faith, in the tears and smiles of those around us, in the baffling moral and social problems of our day, *and* of course in the love of God for his own sake as the sun whose rays penetrate all things.

Secondly, the hardness of the quest for God in our very secular and irreligious society means that we, who live in it alongside our unbelieving neighbours, cannot look for tidy and finished achievements. The working out of our love for God in the life of society is perpetually untidy, unfinished and without a resting-place, all the more so because the framework of thought and sensibility which one could recognize as a Christian art or skill no longer exists. It is therefore too unsettling for our natural taste. But it is the row given us to hoe all the same, and we have no other.

Thirdly, there is, then, all the greater need for a style of allegiance to God which is happy to rest on hope, and on the conviction that God who has shown himself in Jesus accepts us and surrounds us with his gracious love. In that sense, our deficiencies are taken care of.

I am not sure that I can easily point to H P Liddon, whose memory we recall, as an obvious champion of the uncloistered and all-embracing spirituality which I urge. But I can certainly point to Charles Gore, who lived in this place and who both followed Liddon and expanded his vision. In 1896, he preached a sermon on the text, 'My kingdom is not of this world', and he too took it as teaching the very opposite of Bishop Hoadley's message. 'Jesus Christ', he said, 'is really the Saviour and Redeemer of mankind, in its social as well as its individual life, and in the present world as well as in that which is to come.' He might have added that a Christian commitment that attends to 'the soul' in isolation is self-defeating. But a Christian commitment not rooted in attention to God is without direction and purpose, and will dissipate and fade.

For Liddon House Sunday, at the Grosvenor Chapel,
London, November 1985

18

The End of the Gospel

JOHN 21.1–14

———

You know the stock advice given to students on the subject of essay writing: make sure you give it a beginning, a middle, and an end. It is much less jejune and more profound than it sounds. But suppose you cannot decide what the end should be. Gospels in the early Church were not exactly private productions, like student essays are supposed to be. They each had an author, certainly, but they wrote, surely, out of the close fellowship of some congregation or other and wrote for that congregation's needs. No sooner had they written than their work became church property, even to the extent of its being open to improvement or at any rate adaptation to new circumstances.

So: the Gospel of John ends twice over. It is clear that it was first of all meant to stop at the end of chapter twenty: 'Now Jesus did many other signs in the presence of his disciples, which are not written in this book; but these are written that you may believe that Jesus is the Messiah, the Son of God, and that believing you may have life in his name' (John 20.30f.). That is entirely satisfactory, and you certainly do not expect to turn over and find: 'After this Jesus revealed himself again to the disciples by the Sea of Tiberias' (John 21.1). But that is what you do find; and chapter twenty-one goes on for twenty-five verses, and has a nice ending of its own which once more rounds off the book perfectly properly. So it is the usual thing to call chapter twenty-one an appendix and it is commonly thought to be the work of someone other than the writer of the rest; someone who, while of similar outlook, felt he had more to say and who was unwilling to let the original ending do its work (though he did not scratch it out). What was the original ending became just another marker on the way, a final pause for breath.

Now you might say that there is nothing very important in this. The book is church property and a fellow-Christian of the author (or it *may* indeed be the author himself) thinks of more that should be told. So he proceeds to add it. It is all straightforward and above board. But at the very least, he has decided to ignore the original ending; and that, whether he realized it or not, is a serious thing to do – at least as serious, as potentially untidy and confusing, for an evangelist as for the writer of student essays. To do it takes a certain mentality, it takes someone prepared to go further, to upset things for the sake of achieving some supposed good.

In the case of the Gospel of John, it certainly created confusion and untidiness. Chapter twenty centres on Jerusalem; it tells of Jesus appearing to his followers there after his resurrection; and it gives a neat impression that in Jerusalem the Church is to be based – just as it is in the Gospel of Luke and its sequel the Acts of the Apostles. Yet now, in this extra chapter, we read of Jesus appearing to disciples in Galilee. It spoils the pattern and disturbs the harmony. What had come to rest goes off again into unsettling new activity.

In all this, there is something not just about the mentality of those who write and handle books, but about the mentality of religious, more specifically, Christian people. In the case of those who produced the Gospel of John the two roles coincide. We too are Christian people and their work may help us to know our own Christian make-up better and foster its growth in certain directions.

At the risk of a little exaggeration, we may say that the writer of the first twenty chapters of the Gospel of John was a model instance of the tutor's doctrine: he gave a beginning, a middle, and an end, no doubt at all. For him, that whole stood secure, something which was now behind, something to look back to, depend on and use. If one wanted to know where one stood, there it was, there in his book; the Christian truth as he saw it and bequeathed it was summed up. His book and also the Church's book. Like any author's book, his work once written floated away from him, and in its own sphere, in this case the circles for which it was written, began to become an authority. It acquired, or had the possibility of acquiring, rock-like status. So faith, once a fluid and a growing thing, going on in Christian minds and hearts (including that of the author when he had not yet written his book), now looked outside those minds and hearts and back to the book, the authority, with its nice, rounded ending. The object, the book, somewhat replaced the person, the believer, and took the weight off him. The past, a book once written, replaced the present in which faith and life go on. That is a major shift of focus.

You could put it by saying that formerly Christian faith was a kind of conversation, an intertwining of the story of Jesus, remembered and reflected on in believers' minds, and their own personal stories – their lives, reflecting his life and death, being nourished and formed by that as they saw in it richer and fresh meaning. Then came the book, and faith could escape from that fluidity, gain stability and certainty in a world where there was a risk that anyone's view might prevail, anyone's reflections, however weird, claim a hearing.

Then came the writer of chapter twenty-one. Not very much and only temporarily, but still in principle decisively, he disturbed the peace, upset the apple-cart, reintroduced the conversation, the intertwining. For he was saying: This is how it looks to me, I want this too to be known. What he did not do, of course, was to refrain from an ending altogether; he merely gave his own new one. His contribution does not point on towards the future in a series of dots: it ends, plainly. Yet in principle his work was only an interruption in the process: new meanings and interpretations would always be possible and continually arise. But like most of us, he thought he knew where final truth should be found – he just put it in his own new form, giving his own new, quite definite ending.

Christians always have a choice, or perhaps they are hopelessly predisposed, between two directions. They can say that the story has had its ending, the truth has been given once for all. It is for us only to receive it, rely on it, live by it. It is a common view, a reassuring view, and unbelievably venerable. It has been dominant through most of Christian history. (And the realist might note how convenient it has always been to those in authority if they hold the ring that bounds legitimate interpretation.) Yet a study of that history scarcely supports it, for despite all intention, faith has continually adapted itself to new circumstances, revealed new facets, shown new vitality – and ignored old endings.

So Christians can say instead that the story never has an ending, that Jesus initiated a never-ending conversation, his story intertwining with each of our stories, and with our complex corporate stories, uniting us with contemporaries and with the past. That means movement and growth in faith, in the way we apprehend God and the way we relate to him – and receive his gift. It means there is no treachery if we find faith must be for us not the same as it was for our predecessors, and not the same for me at sixty as it was for me at twenty.

The 'ending' lies ever ahead, and it is not for us to speculate about. Only we are to trust, continually trust that it will be for good and for delight. That end is God himself, and nothing else will suffice.

For St John's College, Oxford, May 1984

19

The Gospel and the End

———

Advent faces the preacher – faces the Christian – with a dire choice. For it is centred traditionally on thoughts concerning the End of the World, which compel you to make decisions. You can say that those ideas are, however thrilling or striking, downright misleading; or you can say that they are, when rightly ordered, crucial for grasping what life is about. Let us take the two possibilities in turn.

First, the possibility that Advent is a mistake. How would you come to that conclusion? You could work from passages in the Bible such as are commonly read at this season. They testify to a vision of a wonderful future which was shared by most of those who wrote the New Testament and, in various ways, by many of those behind the Old Testament. One day, said the prophets, God would bring to an end the miseries and horrors of life as it is and renew the world in peace, prosperity and love. Well, says the realist, he never has; and as we read their words, they remain like a dream which we know will pass from our minds, even before we leave the liturgy in which we have heard them. The first Christians shared that Old Testament vision, but now with urgent and often highly coloured hope. Jesus had been among them, had lived and died. He had preached the coming of God's great day and it would not be long delayed. Now, said his early followers, it will soon be with us, and he will return in glory. It did not happen. But their words have lingered in the Church, eventually settling down to be read once a year at Advent, testifying to a hope that once was lived all the year; a hope revived indeed by sects from time to time, but always dashed, and seeming now, if taken at all literally, outlandish, almost unimaginable – though applied, by some who should know better, to political events on the world scene in misjudgments that could warp discretion catastrophically.

That is the first possibility, and I hope you feel it as you listen to the apocalyptic Advent scriptures read; or do they wash over you like soothing water, perfumed with a nostalgic scent you cannot quite identify? They deserve a more vigorous reaction than that!

What about the second possibility? That the thoughts of Advent are crucial for grasping what life is about. When that early Christian hope of the End of the present world order and of Jesus' return failed, eventually most Christians turned to a simple but sad solution. They just put the whole thing off to a more or less distant future. Meantime, the whole temperature of Christian life dropped, in this crucial respect; hope became a duller virtue than faith or love; and life became more on this world's terms, with the Church as an institution within society. The Advent hope was overshadowed, you might say, by the Advent bazaar.

But not all Christians reacted in that way. Others said: Yes, the End is not yet; but we need not look only to heaven and the future for the things of God. Is not the legacy of Jesus here and now among us? Do we not know in our worship and life together the fullness of God's presence? Is not Christ present with us in life and word and sacrament? Do we not carry in our own lives, in our love and witness and fellowship, the reality of God's new world? We must look, not only up or outside to some extraordinary future, but down and within, to the present truth of God and what he has done for us through Jesus. And we can trust that he will do more: if we walk with him, we shall more and more know his gifts and his truth. So we must live expectant – open-eyed, open-mouthed, like young birds in the nest, ready for boundless gifts. So within the tired old world, the new world truly comes to life: and we are its citizens, walking its invisible streets and singing already the songs of Zion.

There have always been Christians, both saints and sectarians, who have felt and believed like that – and I trust that, in our own mode, we may be counted among them. Some (perhaps most) move uneasily between the first kind of Christian reaction that I outlined and this second one. My belief is that you should choose one or the other and stick to it.

There is one further aspect, something not open to the first Christians or indeed to anyone until quite recently. We can now see that the imagery and the language of the very early days, the language we find in Scripture about the coming End, was a kind of poetry. It was not (whatever account its users might have given of it) literal, factual language. It was the way Jews of Jesus' time clothed in words their trust in God, their fervent hope and confidence that, despite appearances, he would indeed act to fulfil his promises. Not unnaturally, Christians inherited that style of poetry and some took it up with gusto. But they knew something much deeper. They knew that in the simple preacher of Galilee who had died on a cross, all that extravagant and fervent hope had somehow begun to find fulfilment and taken identifiable shape. If you really wanted to live by the truth of things, it was on him that you should fix your eyes; and looking to him, long and hard, you would find the path of life and the sweetness of God. If you can share that trust, then you can grasp their hand, across the many centuries and across the cultures, for you share the essence of their faith; and the mood of Advent is something to absorb into yourself and to keep.

Viewed like that, the old Bible poetry falls into place. It is much more than a matter of saving something from the wreckage of an obsolete idiom of thought. Take it literally, and all you do is be mystified, and in practice you shelve the whole subject. Worse still, you miss its deeper message: that our God is all and claims our minds and hearts; that, despite all appearances, hope must spring eternal, in him and because of him; that in Jesus, that hope is pin-pointed, and that grace can enter when we show even a chink of readiness, a gesture of expectancy.

For St George's, Paris, November 1983